Coyright © 2024

All rights reserved. No part of this publication may be reproduced, distributed, or transmitted in any form or by any means, including photocopying, recording, or other electronic or mechanical methods, without the prior written permission of the publisher, except in the case of brief quotations embodied in critical reviews and certain other noncommercial uses permitted by copyright law.

Sammy has always dreamed of exploring space, and now he's getting his chance! Selected for a school space mission simulation, Sammy's adventure takes him to a mysterious planet with an incredible secret. What will he discover, and will his dream of becoming an astronaut come true? Get ready for a fun.

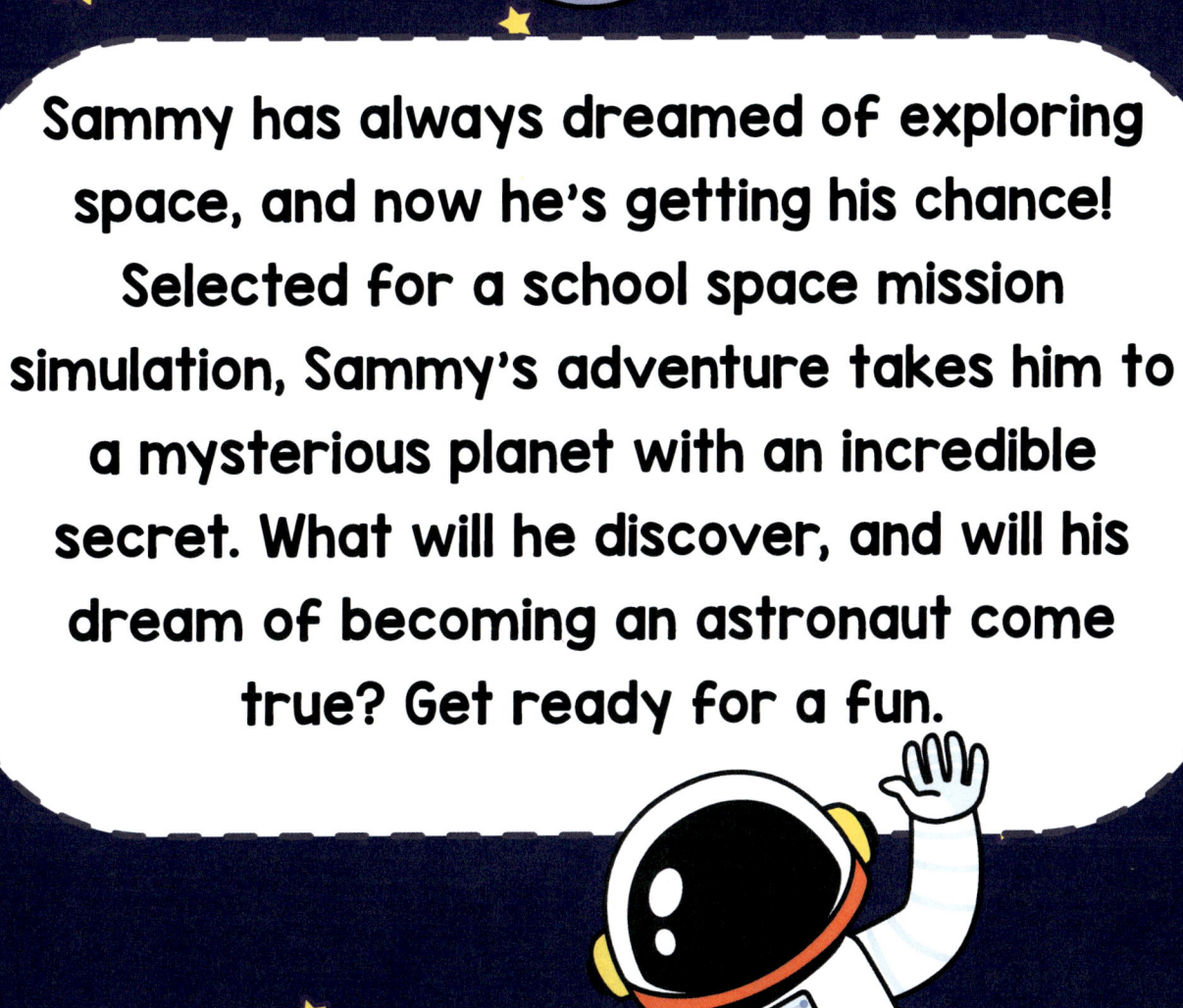

THE BIG DREAM

Sammy loved everything about space. His room was filled with posters of planets, stars, and rockets. He dreamed of one day becoming an astronaut and exploring the galaxy. Every night, before bed, Sammy would stare out of his window, imagining himself flying among the stars.

One day at school, Sammy's teacher announced an exciting event: the school would hold a space mission simulation! Students would get a chance to experience what it was like to be an astronaut. Sammy's heart raced as the teacher explained that only a few students would be chosen to participate.

A few days later, the names of the chosen students were announced. Sammy held his breath as the teacher called out the names. "Sammy!" she said. Sammy couldn't believe it—he was chosen! He felt a mix of excitement and nervousness, but he knew this was his chance to live his dream.

TRAINING FOR SPACE

The next day, the space mission training began. Sammy and the other students learned about spacesuits, rocket ships, and how to float in zero gravity. They even practiced communication, just like real astronauts, by talking to each other through headsets while pretending to be on a space mission.

The space mission simulation wasn't just fun—it was also full of challenges. Sammy and his team had to solve puzzles, fix "broken" parts of the spacecraft, and work together to make sure their imaginary mission was a success. Sammy felt more confident with every task they completed.

After days of training, the final mission simulation was about to begin. Sammy put on his astronaut suit and helmet, feeling a bit nervous but ready for the challenge. His friends cheered him on, and he couldn't wait to start the mission. He was about to embark on the greatest adventure of his life!

THE MYSTERIOUS PLANET

Sammy's final mission simulation had begun, but this time, it was different. He was on a solo adventure, just like a real astronaut on a daring exploration. His ship's control panel beeped, and the screen displayed a mysterious planet—one that no one had ever seen before. "This is my chance to make a new discovery!" Sammy thought as he prepared to land on the unknown planet.

As soon as the ship touched down, Sammy stepped out onto the planet's surface, feeling a sense of adventure and wonder. The ground beneath his boots was unlike anything he had ever seen. It was smooth, shiny, and the air had a warm, cheesy scent. Sammy couldn't help but smile as he noticed hills in the distance that looked like they were made of melted cheese.

Sammy crouched down to examine the ground closely. He reached out and scooped up a small piece of the planet's surface. His eyes widened in disbelief—it was cheese! Real, creamy cheese! He took a deep breath and laughed, "I've discovered a planet made of cheese!" Sammy couldn't believe his luck. He was the first explorer to find such a silly, wonderful planet, and it was all his discovery.

A DREAM COME TRUE

Back in the classroom, Sammy is sitting at his desk, smiling dreamily as he looks at a drawing of the cheese planet he made. Around him, his classmates are chatting and laughing, some sharing their own simulation experiences. The teacher is standing at the front, with space posters on the walls and a model of the solar system hanging from the ceiling.

A group of kids sitting together on the playground during recess. Sammy is in the center, animatedly telling his friends all about the cheese planet. Some kids are pretending to be astronauts, while others are pointing at the sky, imagining their own space adventures. The playground has space-themed murals, with stars, rockets, and planets.

Sammy is lying in his bed at night, staring up at the starry sky through his window. His room is cozy, with space-themed decor like rocket models and planet posters. The moon is shining brightly outside, and Sammy's face shows a peaceful smile, dreaming of the stars and his future adventures in space

What is Sammy's biggest dream?

A. To become a pilot

B. To become an astronaut

C. To become a scientist

What special event is announced at Sammy's school?

A. A space mission simulation
B. A planetarium visit
C. A science fair

What does Sammy bring back from the mysterious planet?

A. A rock

B. A piece of cheese

C. A flower

What do Sammy's friends do when they taste the cheese from the planet?

A. They laugh and enjoy it
B. They say it tastes bad
C. They don't believe Sammy

Made in the USA
Monee, IL
30 March 2025